31 New ATARI Computer Programs

For Home, School, Office

31 New ATARI Computer Programs For Home, School, Office

by Alan North

ARCsoft Publishers
Woodsboro, Maryland

FIRST EDITION
SECOND PRINTING

Printed in the United States of America

Library of Congress LC number: 82-18412

ISBN 0-86668-018-7

Preface

ATARI is one of the world's most-popular computer systems for use in the home, classroom and small-business office. If it's not already more popular than others, it is fast becoming so.

Its lightweight desktop design and powerful language capability place it in the forefront of the new wave of personal computers for hobbyists, students, teachers, professionals, business persons and all who want to learn the technology.

It's not a toy! Its hardware and software combination make it a highly useful tool in the business environment and the classroom as well as for practical jobs around the home.

The total number of applications to which the ATARI computer can be put is limited only by the scope of the imagination. In this book we have attempted to create and share 31 new, specific, practical sets of applications for your use.

This book, as are all published by *ARCsoft Publishers,* is written for newcomers, beginners, novices and first-timers, as well as advanced users of micro-computers. Our intention has been to provide easy-to-type-in-and-run programs for the ATARI Model 400 and Model 800 computers. You type them in and your ATARI does the rest.

This book is a companion volume to *101 ATARI Computer Programming Tips & Tricks.*

—Alan North

Table of Contents

Programs for the business person

Appendix

Introduction

There's a great need for practical, useful software for the new generation of popular personal computers. The ATARI Model 400 and Model 800 computers, for example, are among the world's most popular gear. The ATARI is powerful and versatile and flexible—but what can it do? Once you've purchased the hardware, you need down-to-earth workable programs to run the computer.

The aim of this book is to provide 31 complete, easy-to-type, ready-to-run new and different sets of program lists for you to use in making your ATARI computer work for you.

These programs are useful in themselves. They also make good starting points for further development as you learn more about how to program your own computer. You can use these fun and practical programs and then modify them and expand them to suit your needs as they grow.

These programs are designed to be typed in, just as you find them in the book, with no other programming needed. We assume you have looked over the owner's manual which came with your Model 400 or Model 800

ATARI computer and know how to hook it to your TV set, turn it on and type in programs. You *do not have to be a programmer* to use these pieces of software. Just type them in as you find them here and run them. They will work!

To make sure there are no errors in these programs, we have written and tested each and every one on our own ATARI computer and printed them for reproduction in this book. The ATARI computer operated a line printer and listed these programs. No human hands came between the computer and the listing so no re-typing or proofreading errors have been introduced. You should find these programs will run exactly as reproduced here.

If, after typing in a program, you get an error message from your ATARI computer, check the handy list of error messages and ATARI BASIC words in the Appendix at the rear of this book. Then compare your typed program lines with the lines in this book. Undoubtedly, you will find you have made a typo in entering the program lines into your ATARI. However, should you find an error in a program in this book, please call it to the attention of the author by sending a postcard or letter to him in care of *ARCsoft Publishers,* P.O. Box 132, Woodsboro, MD 21798 USA. He will appreciate being able to make any necessary corrections to future editions.

Home, school and office

The book has been organized into three sections plus the Appendix. The first section includes programs which might seem most useful in the home or wherever hobbyists use a computer. The second section includes programs for use in a learning environment, by students and teachers. This might be a classroom or it might be in your home. The third section holds programs of interest to business persons and professionals.

Naturally, these sections, as divided, are not rigid and exclusive. You probably will find something in the business or classroom section applicable to your home use. And you probably will take several of the home programs to your office or classroom.

Try them all. They're great fun to run. And they are especially designed to be short so you won't have to spend hours typing in one program.

REMarks

As you read through the 31 programs in this book, you will notice few REM, or remarks, statements. The author's training in writing BASIC-language computer programs included an emphasis on brevity and saving memory space. A sharp editing pencil was in order—and still is!

REMarks and explanations in software are out. Honing, fine-tuning and waste trimming are in. Use of coding form program-writing worksheets, such as the *ATARI Computer BASIC Coding Form* tablet published by *ARCsoft Publishers,* is encouraged. The objective always should be to make the most efficient use of available memory.

Always remember: even though they may be headed toward the same goal, no two programmers will write exactly the same list of BASIC instructions, or program lines, from scratch. As you load these 31 programs into your ATARI computer, one at a time, you'll make modifications to suit your personal needs and interests. Exact wording of PRINT statements, for instance, can be changed. Or two or more programs can be combined into one grand scheme. Your applications may vary.

If you want to load more than one of these programs into your ATARI computer at the same time, be sure to use different sets of line numbers for different programs.

RETURN vs. ENTER

Computer programmers today generally mix the two words, RETURN and ENTER, together and use them to mean the same thing. In either case, we mean the button on the right-hand side of the ATARI keyboard printed RETURN.

These programs will run on any computer which is

programmed in BASIC. However, to run on machines, other than the Model 400 and Model 800 by ATARI, you will have to make slight modifications to program lines. Graphics commands, especially, will differ elsewhere.

Refer to the owner's manual which came with your personal computer to compare its version of BASIC with the ATARI BASIC. A handy list of ATARI's BASIC words can be found in the Appendix at the end of this book.

Also, if you use a computer, other than the ATARI 400 or 800, such things as line numbering, logical tests, multiplication symbols, print statements and other instructions may differ.

Special note: screen clear and buzzer

We have attempted to make this book as accurate as possible by reproducing the programs directly from a line-printer printout of the ATARI's program memory. The line printer is unable to reproduce the odd, special "crooked arrow" symbol used by the ATARI video display to represent screen clear or buzzer. Rather, in this book, the right-pointing bracket symbol (}) replaces the crooked arrow. So, if you see a line which reads like this:

10 PRINT "}"

take that to mean either a video display screen clear command or a ring-the-buzzer command.

In most all cases we have placed a REM note immediately after such a command so you know what is being called for. As an example, you might see a line such as this:

10 PRINT "}":REM SCREEN CLEAR

You obtain the crooked arrow by pressing the ESC key and the SHIFT key and the CLEAR key. Press ESC. Then press SHIFT and hold it and press CLEAR. This places the crooked arrow on the screen. To type the full program line above, key in the line number, 10, and the word PRINT and the first quotation mark. Then press ESC, press and hold SHIFT, and press CLEAR. Then key in the final quotation mark. This will write the clear-the-screen command as a program line.

To write a sound-the-buzzer command as a program

line, substitute the 2 key for the CLEAR key used above. Here's a sample program line:

10 PRINT "}":REM BUZZER

To enter this program line, key in the line number, the word PRINT, and the first quotation mark. Then press ESC, press and hold SHIFT and press the 2 key. Then key in the final quotation mark and any other following parts of the line. This will cause the computer to make its buzzing sound effect when it encounters that particular line during a run.

All other letters, numbers and symbols used in this book are found on the ATARI keyboard. In the *Areas* programs, and certain others, where the value of Pi was called for, we have substituted the simple number 3.14 for the value. If you require more accuracy, please feel free to substitute a Pi value to more decimal places.

Endless running

Many of the programs in this book will continue to run until you command them off via the BREAK key. You may stop any run, at any time, with the BREAK key. For example, *Poetrywriter* will continue to generate new and different verses until you press the BREAK key.

The author would like to have your suggestions for changes in future editions of this work, or for other books in this series for the ATARI computers. He may be addressed in care of *ARCsoft Publishers.*

Programs for the home

Horoscope

This fun program will entertain your family and friends for hours. It makes a great party game, too.

The player, or user, talks with the computer, giving his name, month of birth and date of birth. The computer then tells the player his sign of the zodiac and what it means. The computer describes the player's personality and predicts the player's future.

If you find the program a bit long to type in, shorten it by using the sign-of-the-zodiac response only. For instance, between lines 700 and 790 you could delete 710 and 750 or 720 to 750. That would make the program shorter and easier to type in, but without most of the exciting description.

Try it. You'll like it!

Program Listing

```
10 DIM N$(20),M$(9),KY$(1)
20 PRINT "}":REM CLEAR SCREEN
30 PRINT :PRINT "WHAT'S YOUR NAME"
40 INPUT N$
50 PRINT "HI, ";N$;", NICE TO MEET YOU"
60 PRINT
70 PRINT "IN WHAT MONTH WERE YOU BORN"
80 INPUT M$
90 PRINT :PRINT M$;" IS A NICE MONTH"
100 PRINT "WHAT DATE IN ";M$
110 INPUT D
120 PRINT
200 IF M$="DECEMBER" AND D>21 THEN 700
210 IF M$="JANUARY" AND D<20 THEN 700
220 IF M$="JANUARY" AND D>19 THEN 800
230 IF M$="FEBRUARY" AND D<19 THEN 800
240 IF M$="FEBRUARY" AND D>18 THEN 900
250 IF M$="MARCH" AND D<21 THEN 900
260 IF M$="MARCH" AND D>20 THEN 1000
270 IF M$="APRIL" AND D<20 THEN 1000
280 IF M$="APRIL" AND D>19 THEN 2000
290 IF M$="MAY" AND D<21 THEN 2000
```

```
300 IF M$="MAY" AND D>20 THEN 3000
310 IF M$="JUNE" AND D<21 THEN 3000
320 IF M$="JUNE" AND D>20 THEN 4000
330 IF M$="JULY" AND D<23 THEN 4000
340 IF M$="JULY" AND D>22 THEN 5000
350 IF M$="AUGUST" AND D<23 THEN 5000
360 IF M$="AUGUST" AND D>22 THEN 6000
370 IF M$="SEPTEMBER" AND D<24 THEN 6000
380 IF M$="SEPTEMBER" AND D>23 THEN 7000
390 IF M$="OCTOBER" AND D<24 THEN 7000
400 IF M$="OCTOBER" AND D>23 THEN 8000
410 IF M$="NOVEMBER" AND D<22 THEN 8000
420 IF M$="NOVEMBER" AND D>21 THEN 9000
430 IF M$="DECEMBER" AND D<22 THEN 9000
440 CLR :GOTO 10
500 PRINT :PRINT
510 PRINT "TO DO ANOTHER, PRESS RETURN"
520 INPUT KY$
530 CLR :GOTO 10
700 PRINT "SO, ";N$;" YOU'RE CAPRICORN"
710 PRINT "CAPRICORN IS THE GOAT"
720 PRINT "YOU ARE TOUGH HEAD-TO-HEAD."
730 PRINT "YOU MISTRUST PEOPLE BUT"
740 PRINT "YOU LIKE SMALL CHILDREN."
750 PRINT "YOU WILL TAKE A TRIP."
790 GOTO 500
800 PRINT N$;" YOU ARE AN AQUARIUS"
810 PRINT "AQUARIUS IS THE WATER BEARER"
820 PRINT "YOU ARE A LIQUID PERSON."
830 PRINT "YOU DO SNEAKY THINGS BUT"
840 PRINT "PEOPLE SECRETLY ADMIRE YOU."
850 PRINT "YOU SOON WILL FIND A REWARD."
890 GOTO 500
900 PRINT "SO, ";N$;" YOU ARE A PISCES"
910 PRINT "PISCES IS THE FISH"
920 PRINT "YOU OFTEN FEEL WEAK BUT"
930 PRINT "PEOPLE THINK YOU OTHERWISE."
940 PRINT "A STRANGER SOON"
950 PRINT "WILL AFFECT YOUR LIFE."
990 GOTO 500
1000 PRINT "SO, ";N$;" YOU ARE AN ARIES"
```

```
1010 PRINT "ARIES IS THE RAM"
1020 PRINT "YOU SOMETIMES FEEL DEVILISH"
1030 PRINT "BUT OTHERS THINK OF YOU"
1040 PRINT "AS A SAINT."
1050 PRINT "AVOID MOUNTAINS AND CAVES !"
1090 GOTO 500
2000 PRINT "SO, ";N$;" YOU ARE A TAURUS"
2010 PRINT "TAURUS IS THE BULL"
2020 PRINT "MOST OF THE TIME"
2030 PRINT "YOU ARE COMPLETELY HONEST"
2040 PRINT "BUT OTHERS THINK YOU ARE"
2050 PRINT "FULL OF BULL."
2060 PRINT "A NICE FRIEND WILL VISIT."
2090 GOTO 500
3000 PRINT "SO, ";N$;" YOU ARE A GEMINI"
3010 PRINT "GEMINI IS THE TWINS"
3020 PRINT "IT'S HARD FOR YOU TO DECIDE"
3030 PRINT " YOU OFTEN SPLIT A DECISION"
3040 PRINT "YOU SEE TWO SIDES BUT"
3050 PRINT "FRIENDS FIND YOU DECISIVE"
3060 PRINT "AVOID NEWSPAPER REPORTERS !"
3090 GOTO 500
4000 PRINT "SO, ";N$;" YOU ARE A CANCER"
4010 PRINT "CANCER IS THE CRAB"
4020 PRINT "YOU LIKE TO VENT YOUR"
4030 PRINT "FEELINGS WHEN THINGS"
4040 PRINT "GO WRONG AND FRIENDS"
4050 PRINT "SOMETIMES EXCLUDE YOU"
4060 PRINT "JEWELS WILL BE IN YOUR PATH"
4090 GOTO 500
5000 PRINT "OKAY, ";N$;" YOU ARE A LEO"
5010 PRINT "LEO IS THE LION"
5020 PRINT "YOUR ROAR IS WORSE"
5030 PRINT "THAN YOUR BITE."
5040 PRINT "YOUR FRIENDS THINK"
5050 PRINT "YOU ARE A PUSSYCAT."
5060 PRINT "FUR IS IN YOUR FUTURE."
5090 GOTO 500
6000 PRINT "SO, ";N$;" YOU ARE A VIRGO"
6010 PRINT "VIRGO IS THE VIRGIN"
6020 PRINT "CLEANLINESS IS YOUR VIRTUE."
6030 PRINT "CASUAL ASSOCIATES"
```

```
6040 PRINT "THINK YOU ARE TIGHT"
6050 PRINT "BUT THOSE CLOSE TO YOU"
6060 PRINT "KNOW BETTER !"
6070 PRINT "AVOID CARS, BARS AND STARS."
6090 GOTO 500
7000 PRINT "SO, ";N$;" YOU ARE A LIBRA"
7010 PRINT "LIBRA IS THE BALANCE"
7020 PRINT "EVERYTHING WORKS OUT FOR"
7030 PRINT "YOU IN THE END BUT PERILS"
7040 PRINT "ALONG THE WAY SOMETIMES"
7050 PRINT "SEEM TOO GREAT."
7060 PRINT "YOU WILL FIND THE TRUTH."
7090 GOTO 500
8000 PRINT "SO, ";N$;" YOU'RE A SCORPIO"
8010 PRINT "SCORPIO IS THE SCORPION"
8020 PRINT "YOU ARE TRUSTWORTHY, LOYAL,"
8030 PRINT "HELPFUL,FRIENDLY,"
8040 PRINT "COURTEOUS,KIND,OBEDIENT,"
8050 PRINT "CHEERFUL,THRIFTY"
8060 PRINT "AND SEXY."
8070 PRINT "YOU WILL WIN."
8090 GOTO 500
9000 PRINT "WELL, ";N$;", A SAGITTARIUS"
9010 PRINT "SAGITTARIUS IS THE ARCHER"
9020 PRINT "YOU FIRE FROM THE HIP"
9030 PRINT "BUT FRIENDS LIKE YOU ANYWAY"
9040 PRINT "HAPPINESS WILL BE YOURS"
9050 PRINT "BUT WATCH OUT FOR FALSENESS"
9090 GOTO 500
9999 END
```

Monthly Loan Payment

Here's a fast computation of the monthly payment on a loan. The amount borrowed, the principle, is stored in memory location P. I is the annual interest rate and N is the number of payments. I is converted to a monthly interest rate and then to a decimal in line 50.

Program Listing

```
10 PRINT "}":REM CLEAR SCREEN
20 PRINT "AMOUNT BORROWED $ ";:INPUT P
30 PRINT "ANNUAL INTEREST % ";:INPUT I
40 PRINT "NUMBER OF PAYMENTS ";:INPUT N
50 I=0.01*(I/12)
60 M=(P*I)/(1-((1+I)^(-N)))
70 PRINT
80 PRINT "MONTHLY PAYMENT IS $";M
90 PRINT :PRINT :PRINT
100 GOTO 20
```

Sample Run

```
AMOUNT BORROWED $10000
ANNUAL INTEREST % 14
NUMBER OF PAYMENTS 48

MONTHLY PAYMENT IS $273.264871
```

Number Of Days In A Month

Here's a cute teacher for your elementary-age kids. This program displays the name of a month and asks how many days in that month. If the correct number of days is entered, the computer says "correct." If an incorrect number of days is entered, the computer says "wrong." In either case, the correct answer is displayed. The educational game can go on forever if needed.

Program Listing

```
10 PRINT "}":REM CLEAR SCREEN
15 DIM S$(9),C$(2),D$(2)
20 DATA JANUARY,31
30 DATA FEBRUARY,28
40 DATA MARCH,31
50 DATA APRIL,30
60 DATA MAY,31
```

```
70 DATA JUNE,30
80 DATA JULY,31
90 DATA AUGUST,31
100 DATA SEPTEMBER,30
110 DATA OCTOBER,31
120 DATA NOVEMBER,30
130 DATA DECEMBER,31
140 R=INT(100*(RND(1)))
150 IF R>24 THEN 140
160 IF INT(R/2)=R/2 THEN R=R-1
170 FOR L=1 TO R
180 READ S$
190 NEXT L
200 PRINT "MONTH IS ";S$
210 READ C$
220 PRINT "HOW MANY DAYS IN ";S$
225 INPUT D$
230 IF D$=C$ THEN PRINT "CORRECT":GOTO 300
240 PRINT "WRONG"
300 PRINT S$;" HAS ";C$;" DAYS"
310 RESTORE
320 PRINT
330 GOTO 140
```

Poetrywriter™

Well, we said it could do *anything*! All you have to do is explain to your computer about adjectives, nouns, verbs and adverbs. Give it a nice little vocabulary. And off it goes, writing poetry.

The vocabulary is held as DATA in lines 20 to 200. The relationship of the words in each of those program lines is important if you want the computer to make sense with proper syntax.

Each DATA line has seven items (after the BASIC word DATA). The seventh "word" actually is a phrase as we use it but is treated as one unit. The seven items are separated by commas.

We use the first English word in the DATA line for

transitions. The second and third English words are adjectives.

The fourth word is a plural noun. The fifth word is a verb. The sixth word is an adverb. And the seventh item is a colorful phrase. It could just as well be a single word.

The computer randomly selects one of each of the seven types of English words and puts them together to form sentences.

Random number generators are in lines 300, 400, 500, 600, 700, 800, and 900. Punctuation and print-out order is determined in lines 1000 to 1100.

The computer will write poems all day until you press its BREAK key.

Program Listing

```
5 PRINT "}":REM CLEAR SCREEN
10 DIM V$(20),W$(20),X$(20),Y$(20)
15 DIM Z$(20),A$(20),B$(20)
20 DATA THE,BIG,BLUE,MARBLES,RUN,
   SMOOTHLY,IN THE SAND
30 DATA WHILE,JOLLY,GREEN,GIANTS,EAT,
   HEARTILY,ON THE HILL
40 DATA AND,FRIENDLY,OLD,BOYS,WEAR,WELL,
   AS THEY AGE
50 DATA OR,HARD,PLASTIC,BUTTONS,LAST,
   TOUGHLY,FOREVER
60 DATA WHEN,HAIRY,TINY,DOGS,PASS,
   RUGGEDLY,IN THE NIGHT
70 DATA FROM,WEALTHY,RED,BAGS,TALK,
   HAPPILY,FROM THE VALLEY
80 DATA FOR,LIVELY,MEAN,FOLKS,PLOW,
   NICELY,ABOVE THE CLOUDS
90 DATA THE,PRETTY,TIMELY,LOVERS,FLY,
   LOOSELY,IN THE GROUND
100 DATA MEANWHILE,SAD,YOUNG,CATS,GRIND,
    CONCRETELY,BEHIND THE BARN
110 DATA FROM,TIRED,POOR,DRINKERS,FLASH,
    BRIGHTLY,IN THE PAN
120 DATA ABOUT,TIGHT,BALD,WIVES,PLAY,
    NOISELY,BEYOND THE PALE
```

```
130 DATA THE,FOLDED,GLOWING,FARMERS,
    SHINE,MERRILY,TOWARD OUR LIVES
140 DATA AND,ROUGH,DARK,HENCHMEN,
    TRYST,SWEETLY,NEAR A TREE
150 DATA AS,TIMELY,ROUND,PRIESTS,FOLLOW,
    BLINDLY,DOWN THE TUBES
160 DATA WHILE,CRUNCHY,BULKY,STATUES,
    LIFT,WETLY,IN THE BOX
170 DATA AND,GOLDEN,SILVERY,BODIES,TURN,
    FREELY,IN THE WIND
180 DATA WHILE,NAKED,CARVED,FLOWERS,GLOW
    ,SMARTLY,FROM A MOUNTAIN
190 DATA WHERE,SPARKLING,LOUD,MEN,FIGHT,
    WHOLEHEARTEDLY,TO THE DEATH
200 DATA AND,FRESH,NEW,ANCIENTS,HUMANIZE,
    BRAZENLY,FOR THE REST
300 R=INT(133*(RND(1)))
310 IF R<7 THEN 300
320 IF INT(R/7)<>(R/7) THEN 300
330 FOR L=1 TO R
340 READ V$
350 NEXT L
360 RESTORE
400 R=INT(133*(RND(1)))
410 IF R<7 THEN 400
420 IF INT(R/7)<>(R/7) THEN 400
430 FOR L=1 TO R-1
440 READ W$
450 NEXT L
460 RESTORE
500 R=INT(133*(RND(1)))
510 IF R<7 THEN 500
520 IF INT(R/7)<>(R/7) THEN 500
530 FOR L=1 TO R-2
540 READ X$
550 NEXT L
560 RESTORE
600 R=INT(133*(RND(1)))
610 IF R<7 THEN 600
620 IF INT(R/7)<>(R/7) THEN 600
630 FOR L=1 TO R-3
```

```
640 READ Y$
650 NEXT L
660 RESTORE
700 R=INT(133*(RND(1)))
710 IF R<7 THEN 700
720 IF INT(R/7)<>(R/7) THEN 700
730 FOR L=1 TO R-4
740 READ Z$
750 NEXT L
760 RESTORE
800 R=INT(133*(RND(1)))
810 IF R<7 THEN 800
820 IF INT(R/7)<>(R/7) THEN 800
830 FOR L=1 TO R-5
840 READ A$
850 NEXT L
860 RESTORE
900 R=INT(133*(RND(1)))
910 IF R<7 THEN 900
920 IF INT(R/7)<>(R/7) THEN 900
930 FOR L=1 TO R-6
940 READ B$
950 NEXT L
960 RESTORE
1000 D=D+1
1010 IF INT(D/2)=D/2 THEN 1030
1020 PRINT A$;" ";Z$;" ";Y$:GOTO 1040
1030 PRINT B$;" ";A$;" ";Z$;" ";Y$
1040 IF INT(D/2)=D/2 THEN 1060
1050 PRINT X$;" ";W$;" ";V$;",":GOTO 1070
1060 PRINT X$;" ";W$;" ";V$;"."
1070 IF INT(D/2)=D/2 THEN PRINT
1080 FOR C=1 TO 100:NEXT C
1090 IF D<12 THEN 300
1100 D=0:PRINT :PRINT :GOTO 300
```

Sample Run

```
SAD TINY CATS
GLOW SMOOTHLY NEAR A TREE,
THE LIVELY GREEN MARBLES
PLOW HAPPILY FOREVER.
```

TIRED TINY STATUES
FIGHT MERRILY ON THE HILL,
WHEN TIGHT YOUNG PRIESTS
RUN WETLY ABOVE THE CLOUDS.

FRIENDLY BLUE LOVERS
FIGHT NOISELY NEAR A TREE,
WHILE FOLDED RED MEN
TALK NOISELY TO THE DEATH.

LIVELY LOUD FOLKS
PASS WELL BEHIND THE BARN,
AS HARD TIMELY DOGS
EAT SMARTLY BEHIND THE BARN.

CRUNCHY MEAN FLOWERS
GLOW HAPPILY BEHIND THE BARN,
WHILE PRETTY POOR GIANTS
TURN BRIGHTLY IN THE NIGHT.

TIGHT POOR FARMERS
TALK SMARTLY DOWN THE TUBES,
WHEN WEALTHY GLOWING DOGS
PASS BRIGHTLY IN THE BOX.

Sample Run

GOLDEN OLD BAGS
FOLLOW WETLY IN THE GROUND,
THE TIRED GREEN BUTTONS
FLASH MERRILY BEHIND THE BARN.

FOLDED BLUE PRIESTS
PLOW RUGGEDLY AS THEY AGE,
THE WEALTHY BLUE LOVERS
PASS TOUGHLY IN THE BOX.

WEALTHY BULKY FARMERS
LAST MERRILY FROM A MOUNTAIN,
WHILE JOLLY RED LOVERS
LAST WHOLEHEARTEDLY BEHIND THE BARN.

```
HARD TINY FOLKS
TALK BRIGHTLY AS THEY AGE,
THE GOLDEN YOUNG BUTTONS
FIGHT HAPPILY IN THE BOX.

FRIENDLY ROUND DOGS
WEAR LOOSELY FROM THE VALLEY,
AS HAIRY LOUD LOVERS
GLOW WHOLEHEARTEDLY IN THE NIGHT.

PRETTY TIMELY BODIES
GRIND FREELY IN THE GROUND,
AS FRIENDLY SILVERY LOVERS
LIFT MERRILY IN THE WIND.
```

High/Low Bowling Score

Suppose you bowl with a group of friends, each with a different score or set of scores? This program accepts their names and scores and sorts out the persons with the highest and the lowest bowling scores.

To complete data entry, simply press RETURN without data. That prompts your computer, via lines 140 and 150, to print the lowest score and the highest score.

Naturally, this kind of sorting could be applied to any game with ranges of scores among different players.

Program Listing

```
10 PRINT "}":REM SCREEN CLEAR
20 DIM N$(20),LN$(20),HN$(20),K$(1)
30 PRINT "}":REM BUZZER
40 PRINT "NAME:",:INPUT N$
50 IF N$="" THEN 120
60 PRINT "SCORE:",:INPUT S
70 X=X+1
80 IF X=1 THEN LS=S:LN$=N$:HS=S:HN$=N$
90 IF S<LS THEN LS=S:LN$=N$
100 IF S>HS THEN HS=S:HN$=N$
```

```
110 GOTO 40
120 PRINT :PRINT
130 PRINT "}":REM BUZZER
140 PRINT "LOWEST SCORE:",LN$,LS
150 PRINT "HIGHEST SCORE:",HN$,HS
160 PRINT :PRINT :PRINT :PRINT
170 PRINT "TO DO MORE, PRESS RETURN"
180 INPUT K$
190 CLR :GOTO 10
```

Sample Run

```
RUN  RETURN
NAME:
JOHN RETURN
SCORE: 50

NAME:
SUSAN RETURN
SCORE:
89 RETURN

NAME:
SCOTT  RETURN
SCORE:
72 RETURN

NAME:
BOB RETURN
SCORE:
67 RETURN

NAME:
TOM RETURN
SCORE:
87 RETURN

NAME:
RETURN

LOWEST SCORE: JOHN 50
HIGHEST SCORE: SUSAN 89
```

Random Number Quality Checker

Ever wonder just how unintentional, haphazard, or unrelated your random numbers are? This program reinforces your confidence in the pseudorandom number generator in the computer.

It causes the machine to generate 100 numbers between zero and 100 and reports how many are above 49 and how many are below 50.

Just for fun, we've thrown in an executive decision maker. That is, the board of directors voted 47 yes, 53 no. Can you imagine it?

Program Listing

```
10 PRINT "}":REM CLEAR SCREEN
20 CLR
30 FOR L=1 TO 100
40 X=INT(100*(RND(1)))
50 IF X<50 THEN Y=Y+1
60 IF X>49 THEN N=N+1
70 NEXT L
80 PRINT "YES:",Y
90 PRINT "NO:",N
100 PRINT
110 GOTO 20
```

Sample Run

```
YES:        48
NO:         52

YES:        58
NO:         42

YES:        50
NO:         50

YES:        54
NO:         46
```

```
YES:        43
NO:         57

YES:        53
NO:         47
```

Super Slot-0

As with all the programs used as examples in this book, simply type this one in and RUN it. The computer will display, on your video screen, the name of this program and some simple instructions.

To simulate pulling the slot machine's lever arm, press the RETURN key on the keyboard.

Program Listing

```
10 PRINT "}":REM CLEAR SCREEN"
20 DIM A$(1),B$(1),C$(1)
30 DIM D$(1),E$(1),K$(1)
40 GOSUB 500
50 PRINT :PRINT
60 GOSUB 200
70 PRINT "***** ***** ***** ***** *****"
80 PRINT "* ";A$;" * * ";B$;" * * ";C$;"
   * * ";D$;" * * ";E$;" *"
90 PRINT "***** ***** ***** ***** *****"
100 PRINT :PRINT :PRINT
110 PRINT "TO PULL LEVER, PRESS RETURN"
120 INPUT K$
130 CLR :GOTO 10
200 GOSUB 400
210 A$=CHR$(X)
220 GOSUB 400
230 B$=CHR$(X)
240 GOSUB 400
250 C$=CHR$(X)
260 GOSUB 400
270 D$=CHR$(X)
```

```
280 GOSUB 400
290 E$=CHR$(X)
300 GOTO 460
400 R=INT(5*(RND(1)))
410 IF R<1 THEN 400
420 IF R=1 THEN X=0
430 IF R=2 THEN X=16
440 IF R=3 THEN X=96
450 IF R=4 THEN X=123
460 RETURN
500 PRINT "      ****************"
510 PRINT "      * ATARI SLOT-O *"
520 PRINT "      ****************"
530 RETURN
```

Savings Quickie

Want a quick idea of how much your savings account will grow over the years? This program is fast to load and speedy to run.

The computer will ask for initial savings balance, annual interest percentage rate, and number of years. In return, it computes compound interest and displays the savings balance at the end of each year in a handy list.

Program Listing

```
10 DIM K$(1)
20 PRINT "}":REM CLEAR SCREEN
30 PRINT "PRESENT SAVINGS BALANCE"
40 INPUT B
50 PRINT "INTEREST RATE"
60 INPUT I
70 PRINT "NUMBER OF YEARS"
80 INPUT Y
90 FOR L=1 TO Y
100 Z=Z+I*(Z+B)/100
110 PRINT L,Z+B
120 NEXT L
200 FOR A=1 TO 4:PRINT :NEXT A
```

```
210 PRINT "TO DO ANOTHER, PRESS RETURN"
220 INPUT K$
230 CLR :GOTO 10
```

Sample Run

```
RUN   RETURN

PRESENT SAVINGS BALANCE:
652   RETURN
INTEREST RATE?
8    RETURN
NUMBER OF YEARS?
11   RETURN

1           704.16
2           760.4928
3           821.332224
4           887.038801
5           958.001905
6           1034.642057
7           1117.413421
8           1206.806494
9           1303.351013
10          1407.619094
11          1520.228621
```

Draw Straws

Here's one of man's oldest decision makers. Several straws are broken off to the same length except for one extra-short straw. The length of all straws is concealed and each person draws a straw. The person drawing the shortest straw "wins." That is, he is selected by the luck of the draw.

Now, your computer can provide a fast and easy drawing where no straws are available. It does all the work for you by assigning electronic straws randomly to each person. Those straws are numbers. The shortest straw, or lowest number, "wins."

Program Listing

```
10 PRINT "}":REM CLEAR SCREEN
20 DIM B$(6),C$(6),D$(6),K$(1)
30 FOR L=1 TO 11:PRINT "*";:NEXT L
40 PRINT
50 PRINT "DRAW STRAWS"
60 FOR L=1 TO 11:PRINT "*";:NEXT L
70 PRINT :PRINT
80 PRINT "PLAYER 1: ";:INPUT B$
90 PRINT "PLAYER 2: ";:INPUT C$
100 PRINT "PLAYER 3: ";:INPUT D$
110 B=INT(100*(RND(1)))
120 L=B
130 C=INT(100*(RND(1)))
140 IF C<L THEN L=C
150 D=INT(100*(RND(1)))
160 IF D<L THEN L=D
170 PRINT
180 PRINT B$;": ",B;
190 IF L=B THEN PRINT " <<<<":GOTO 210
200 PRINT
210 PRINT C$;": ",C;
220 IF L=C THEN PRINT " <<<<":GOTO 240
230 PRINT
240 PRINT D$;": ",D;
250 IF L=D THEN PRINT " <<<<"
300 PRINT :PRINT :PRINT
310 PRINT "FOR MORE, PRESS RETURN"
320 INPUT K$
330 CLR :GOTO 10
```

Funny similes

Give these newfangled gadgets an inch and they'll take a mile. In the case of the computer, give it some tacky retorts and it will spew out an endless string of dumb remarks.

The fun is in having the computer randomly select various words and combine them to make silly sayings.

The random number is used to match the words into similes.

Program Listing

```
10 PRINT "}":REM CLEAR SCREEN
20 DATA SHORT,TALL,FAT,LEAN,CLEAN
30 DATA DIRTY,GOOD,BAD,HAPPY,SAD
40 DATA GREEN,RED,YELLOW,BLUE,UGLY
50 DATA PRETTY,SHARP,DULL,TACKY,NATTY
60 DATA STRONG,WEAK,MEAN,NICE,DUMB
70 DATA GNOME,TREE,PIG,BOX,CLOCK
80 DATA TURKEY,GOLD,APPLE,DOG,ROOKIE
90 DATA BEET,BIRD,SKY,SIN,PEACH
100 DATA TACK,RAZOR,PIN,PLUG,BULL
110 DATA WORM,LION,LAMB,PUPPY,OX
200 DIM B$(10),D$(10),E$(10),K$(1)
210 PRINT "}":REM BUZZER
220 PRINT "WHOM ARE WE DESCRIBING"
230 INPUT B$
300 T=INT(100*(RND(1)))
310 IF T<1 OR T>25 THEN 300
320 FOR L=1 TO T
330 READ D$
340 NEXT L
350 RESTORE
400 T=INT(100*(RND(1)))
410 IF T<26 OR T>50 THEN 400
420 FOR L=1 TO T
430 READ E$
440 NEXT L
450 RESTORE
500 PRINT "}":REM BUZZER
510 PRINT B$;" IS ";D$;" AS A ";E$
600 FOR L=1 TO 8:PRINT :NEXT L
610 PRINT "FOR ANOTHER, PRESS RETURN"
620 INPUT K$
630 CLR :GOTO 10
```

Programs for the classroom

Foreign Capitals

Here's a learning quiz we'll bet you haven't seen anywhere else. This program tests your knowledge of foreign countries. The more you play, the more you learn!

You must tell the computer the correct name of the capital of the country it presents. And you must spell the name of that city correctly.

What is the capital of Egypt, Poland, Turkey, New Zealand, Bolivia or Afghanistan? It can be very tough!

Want to change to different countries? Change the DATA lines 20 to 540. Be sure to put a comma between country and capital in each DATA line.

Program Listing

```
10 PRINT "}":REM CLEAR SCREEN
15 DIM S$(20),C$(20),D$(20)
20 DATA AFGHANISTAN,KABUL
30 DATA ALBANIA,TIRANA
40 DATA ALGERIA,ALGIERS
50 DATA ARGENTINA,BUENOS AIRES
60 DATA AUSTRALIA,CANBERRA
70 DATA AUSTRIA,VIENNA
80 DATA BAHRAIN,MANAMA
90 DATA BANGLADESH,DACCA
100 DATA BELGIUM,BRUSSELS
110 DATA BOLIVIA,LA PAZ
120 DATA BRAZIL,BRASILIA
130 DATA BULGARIA,SOFIA
140 DATA BURMA,RANGOON
150 DATA CHILE,SANTIAGO
160 DATA COLOMBIA,BOGOTA
170 DATA CUBA,HAVANA
180 DATA CZECHOSLOVAKIA,PRAGUE
190 DATA DENMARK,COPENHAGEN
200 DATA EGYPT,CAIRO
210 DATA FINLAND,HELSINKI
220 DATA FRANCE,PARIS
230 DATA GERMANY EAST,EAST BERLIN
```

```
240 DATA GERMANY WEST,BONN
250 DATA GREECE,ATHENS
260 DATA HAITI,PORT-AU-PRINCE
270 DATA HUNGARY,BUDAPEST
280 DATA ICELAND,REYKJAVIK
290 DATA INDIA,NEW DELHI
300 DATA IRAN,TEHRAN
310 DATA ITALY,ROME
320 DATA JAPAN,TOKYO
330 DATA KUWAIT,KUWAIT
340 DATA LIBYA,TRIPOLI
350 DATA MEXICO,MEXICO CITY
360 DATA NEPAL,KATHMANDU
370 DATA NEW ZEALAND,WELLINGTON
380 DATA NORWAY,OSLO
390 DATA OMAN,MUSCAT
400 DATA PERU,LIMA
410 DATA POLAND,WARSAW
420 DATA QATAR,DOHA
430 DATA ROMANIA,BUCHAREST
440 DATA SPAIN,MADRID
450 DATA SUDAN,KHARTOUM
460 DATA SWEDEN,STOCKHOLM
470 DATA SWITZERLAND,BERN
480 DATA TURKEY,ANKARA
490 DATA U.S.S.R.,MOSCOW
500 DATA UNITED KINGDOM,LONDON
510 DATA VENEZUELA,CARACAS
520 DATA YUGOSLAVIA,BELGRADE
530 DATA ZAIRE,KINSHASA
540 DATA ZAMBIA,LUSAKA
550 PRINT "***** FOREIGN CAPITALS *****"
555 PRINT "   HOW MANY CAN YOU NAME?"
560 R=INT(106*(RND(1)))
570 IF R<1 THEN 560
580 IF INT(R/2)=R/2 THEN R=R-1
590 FOR L=1 TO R
600 READ S$
610 NEXT L
620 PRINT :PRINT
630 PRINT "COUNTRY:  ";S$
640 READ C$
```

```
650 PRINT "WHAT IS THE CAPITAL":INPUT D$
660 IF D$=C$ THEN PRINT "RIGHT":GOTO 680
670 PRINT "WRONG"
680 PRINT "CAPITAL OF ";S$;" IS ";C$
690 RESTORE
700 PRINT :PRINT
710 GOTO 560
```

Areas

Circle. Ellipse. Parabola. Sphere. Square. Rectangle. Triangle. Name your shape. This program will compute its area. Surface area in the case of the sphere. Answer the computer's questions and it will give you the answer you need, in square units of measure. If you use inches, the answer will be in square inches. Put in yards and get square yards. Meters, get square meters. Please don't mix units in any one computation.

Program Listing

```
10 PRINT "}":REM CLEAR SCREEN
20 DIM S$(10)
30 PRINT "SHAPE: ";
40 INPUT S$
45 PRINT
50 IF S$="CIRCLE" THEN 100
55 IF S$="ELLIPSE" THEN 200
60 IF S$="PARABOLA" THEN 300
65 IF S$="SPHERE" THEN 400
70 IF S$="SQUARE" THEN 500
75 IF S$="RECTANGLE" THEN 500
80 IF S$="TRIANGLE" THEN 600
90 PRINT :GOTO 30
100 PRINT "RADIUS = ";
110 INPUT R
120 A=3.14*(R^2)
130 GOTO 700
200 PRINT "MAJOR AXIS = ";
```

```
210 INPUT J
220 PRINT "MINOR AXIS = ";
230 INPUT N
240 A=0.7854*J*N
250 GOTO 700
300 PRINT "BASE = ";
310 INPUT B
320 PRINT "HEIGHTH = ";
330 INPUT H
340 A=(2/3)*(B*H)
350 GOTO 700
400 PRINT "RADIUS = ";
410 INPUT R
420 A=3.14*4*(R^2)
430 GOTO 700
500 PRINT "LENGTH = ";
510 INPUT L
520 IF S$="SQUARE" THEN A=L*L:GOTO 700
530 PRINT "WIDTH = ";
540 INPUT W
550 A=L*W
560 GOTO 700
600 PRINT "BASE = ";
610 INPUT B
620 PRINT "HEIGHTH = ";
630 INPUT H
640 A=0.5*B*H
700 PRINT
710 PRINT "AREA = ";A
720 PRINT
730 GOTO 30
```

Sample Run

```
SHAPE:
TRIANGLE
BASE =
55
HEIGHTH =
22
AREA = 605
```

```
SHAPE:
ELLIPSE
MAJOR AXIS =
19
MINOR AXIS =
14
AREA = 208.9164
```

Photography: Flash Exposure

Use your computer to help take better pictures!

The most important factor in pictures shot with flash is the distance from your flash to the subject. Subjects which are close to you will receive a lot of light while subjects farther away will receive less light.

Check your data sheet for the film you are using. Look for the film guide number. Next, make an estimate of the distance in feet from the flash to your subject.

This program determines the proper *f*/stop setting for your camera. By the way, if the computer tells you to use an *f*/stop setting between two *f*/numbers available on your camera, set your lens opening at the nearest *f*/number or halfway between the two, whichever is closest.

For example, suppose your film has a guide number of 80 and you estimate the flash-to-subject distance at 10 feet. Use *f/8* on your lens.

Program Listing

```
10 DIM K$(1)
20 PRINT "}":REM CLEAR SCREEN
30 PRINT "}":REM BUZZER
40 PRINT "PHOTOGRAPHY: FLASH EXPOSURE"
50 PRINT :PRINT
60 PRINT "WHAT IS FILM GUIDE NUMBER"
70 INPUT G
80 PRINT "FLASH-TO-SUBJECT DISTANCE"
90 INPUT D
100 F=G/D
110 PRINT :PRINT
```

```
120 PRINT "}":REM BUZZER
130 PRINT "GUIDE NUMBER: ";G
140 PRINT "DISTANCE:      ";D;" FEET"
150 PRINT "SHOOT AT:      F/";F
160 FOR L=1 TO 6:PRINT :NEXT L
170 PRINT "FOR MORE, PRESS RETURN"
180 INPUT K$
190 CLR :GOTO 10
```

Sample Run

```
PHOTOGRAPHY: FLASH EXPOSURE
WHAT IS FILM GUIDE NUMBER
80          RETURN
FLASH-TO-SUBJECT DISTANCE
10          RETURN

GUIDE NUMBER: 80
DISTANCE:     10 FEET
SHOOT AT:     F/8
```

Photography: Close Ups

For copying and other close-up work with your camera, you extend the camera lens by using bellows or extension tubes. In doing that, you must allow for an effective increase in the normal *f*/number or your picture will be underexposed.

You make such an exposure compensation whenever the subject distance is less than eight times the focal length of your lens.

This program provides a convenient means of determining the effective *f*/number. For example, if the focal length of your camera is 50mm and the lens-to-film distance (focal length plus extension from infinity position) is 100mm, and the normal *f*/stop would be 22, the corrected stop would be *f/11*.

Or, if you are using a 25mm lens, with 50mm lens-to-film distance, a normal *f*/stop of 8 should be corrected to *f/4*. Be sure to keep both focal length and distance in either mm or inches. Don't mix apples and oranges.

Program Listing

```
10 DIM K$(1)
20 PRINT "}":REM CLEAR SCREEN
30 PRINT "}":REM BUZZER
40 PRINT "PHOTOGRAPHY: CLOSE UPS"
50 PRINT :PRINT
60 PRINT "WHAT IS NORMAL F/ NUMBER"
70 INPUT F
80 PRINT "LENS-TO-FILM DISTANCE IN MM"
90 INPUT D
100 IF D=0 THEN 80
110 PRINT "LENS FOCAL LENGTH IN MM"
120 INPUT L
130 N=F*L/D
200 PRINT :PRINT
210 PRINT "}":REM BUZZER
220 PRINT "EFFECTIVE F/NUMBER IS F/";N
300 FOR L=1 TO 6:PRINT :NEXT L
310 PRINT "FOR MORE, PRESS RETURN"
320 INPUT K$
330 CLR :GOTO 10
```

Sample Run

```
PHOTOGRAPHY: CLOSE UPS


WHAT IS NORMAL F/ NUMBER
22              RETURN
LENS-TO-FILM DISTANCE IN MM
100             RETURN
LENS FOCAL LENGTH IN MM
50              RETURN

EFFECTIVE F/ NUMBER IS F/11
```

Math Flasher

Here's the basic routine (no pun intended) for an educational flash-card program. This one is bare-bones, no frills. You can dress it up with more colorful right-n-wrong messages, opening and closing billboards, etc. You could even make it keep score and present a "batting average" at the end of its run.

Here's how it works:

Lines 10 - 90 determine which type of math you wish to do. Lines 50- 80 move program action to the appropriate group of lines further along in the program.

Lines 200-280 handle addition. Lines 300-390, subtraction. Lines 400-480, multiplication. Lines 500-590, division.

For example, look at lines 200-280. Two separate random numbers are generated (lines 200 and 210). The random numbers are labeled P and Q. At line 220, the program uses P and Q and asks you to add them together. Line 230 waits for and accepts your answer.

Line 240 clears old, unwanted words from the screen to reduce confusion. At line 250, the program makes the right or wrong decision, using the powerful IF/THEN statement. Line 270 prints the correct answer.

Program execution for subtract (lines 300-390), multiply (lines 400-480), and divide (lines 500-590), are similar except for line 320 in subtraction and line 520 in division.

We make the assumption that it is not desirable to have negative numbers as results of subtraction. That is, we want only subtraction problems with results of zero, one, two, three, or higher. We want no problems which would result in answers below zero such as -1, -2, -3, and so forth. So, line 320 tests P and Q, before presenting the problem on the screen. If they will result in a negative-number answer, then the program returns to lines 300-310 for two new numbers.

In division, we want whole-number answers. That is, we want answers like 2 or 11 or 26. Not answers like 1.81 or 9.75 or 21.3343. So, line 520 tests P and Q to make sure their dividend will be a whole number. If not, the program goes back to line 500 and line 510 for two new numbers.

Program Listing

```
10 DIM B$(8)
15 PRINT "}":REM CLEAR SCREEN
20 PRINT "DO YOU WANT TO"
25 PRINT "ADD":PRINT "SUBTRACT"
30 PRINT "MULTIPLY":PRINT "DIVIDE"
40 PRINT :PRINT "WHICH":INPUT B$
50 IF B$="ADD" THEN 200
60 IF B$="SUBTRACT" THEN 300
70 IF B$="MULTIPLY" THEN 400
80 IF B$="DIVIDE" THEN 500
90 GOTO 35
200 P=INT(10*(RND(1)))
210 Q=INT(10*(RND(1)))
220 PRINT :PRINT "ADD ";P;" PLUS ";Q
230 INPUT R
240 PRINT "}":REM CLEAR SCREEN
250 IF R=P+Q THEN PRINT "RIGHT":GOTO 270
260 PRINT "WRONG"
270 PRINT P;" PLUS ";Q;" EQUALS ";P+Q
280 FOR LL=1 TO 1000:NEXT LL
290 PRINT :GOTO 200
300 P=INT(10*(RND(1)))
310 Q=INT(10*(RND(1)))
320 IF P-Q<0 THEN 300
325 PRINT
330 PRINT "SUBTRACT ";Q;" FROM ";P
340 INPUT R
350 PRINT "}":REM CLEAR SCREEN
360 IF R=P-Q THEN PRINT "RIGHT":GOTO 380
370 PRINT "WRONG"
380 PRINT P;" MINUS ";Q;" EQUALS ";P-Q
385 FOR LL=1 TO 1000:NEXT LL
390 PRINT :GOTO 300
400 P=INT(10*(RND(1)))
410 Q=INT(10*(RND(1)))
415 PRINT
420 PRINT "MULTIPLY ";P;" TIMES ";Q
```

```
430 INPUT R
440 PRINT "}":REM CLEAR SCREEN
450 IF R=P*Q THEN PRINT "RIGHT":GOTO 470
460 PRINT "WRONG"
470 PRINT P;" TIMES ";Q;" EQUALS ";P*Q
480 FOR LL=1 TO 1000:NEXT LL
490 PRINT :GOTO 400
500 P=INT(100*(RND(1)))
510 Q=INT(10*(RND(1)))
520 IF P/Q<>INT(P/Q) THEN 500
530 PRINT "DIVIDE ";P;" BY ";Q
540 INPUT R
550 PRINT "}":REM CLEAR SCREEN
560 IF R=P/Q THEN PRINT "RIGHT":GOTO 580
570 PRINT "WRONG"
580 PRINT P;"/";Q;"=";P/Q
585 FOR LL=1 TO 1000:NEXT LL
590 PRINT :GOTO 500
```

Exam Score Sorting

The final number scores of a large number of test results can be categorized and thereby cut down into a smaller quantity of numbers easily.

This program accepts exam scores and divides them into ranges we have labeled A, B, C, D and F. The program looks for test scores in a range of zero to 100. The predetermined grade ranges are F=0 to 59; D=60 to 69; C=70 to 79; B=80 to 89; and A=90 to 100.

You key in the letter X to break the entry cycle. Lines 100 to 140 sort the scores into letter grades A through F. Lines 150 to 170 sort highest and lowest scores. Line 200 finds the mid-range and average scores.

Program Listing

```
10 PRINT "}":REM CLEAR SCREEN
15 CLR :DIM G$(3),RT$(1)
20 PRINT "}":REM BUZZER
30 PRINT "ENTER A GROUP OF SCORES,"
40 PRINT "FROM ZERO TO 100,"
45 PRINT "ONE AT  TIME"
50 PRINT
55 PRINT "ENTER X AFTER LAST SCORE"
60 PRINT :PRINT "SCORE:"
65 INPUT G$
70 IF G$="X" THEN 200
80 G=VAL(G$)
90 N=N+1
100 IF G<60 THEN F=F+1:GOTO 150
110 IF G<70 THEN D=D+1:GOTO 150
120 IF G<80 THEN C=C+1:GOTO 150
130 IF G<90 THEN B=B+1:GOTO 150
140 A=A+1
150 IF N=1 THEN L=G:H=G
160 IF G<L THEN L=G
170 IF G>H THEN H=G
180 S=S+G
190 GOTO 60
200 P=S/N:M=L+((H-L)/2)
210 PRINT "}":REM CLEAR SCREEN
215 PRINT "A TOTAL OF ";N;" SCORES"
220 PRINT "RANGING FROM ";L;" TO ";H
230 PRINT "MID-RANGE SCORE IS ";M
240 PRINT "AVERAGE SCORE IS ";P
250 PRINT
255 PRINT "TOTALS FOR EACH LETTER:"
260 PRINT "A: ";A
270 PRINT "B: ";B
280 PRINT "C: ";C
290 PRINT "D: ";D
300 PRINT "F: ";F
310 PRINT :PRINT :PRINT
320 PRINT "TO DO MORE, PRESS RETURN"
330 INPUT RT$
340 GOTO 10
```

Astronomy
Lightyears/Distance Conversions

Starlight,
Starbright,
I wish I may,
I wish I might,
Know the distance
To your light.

For students of astronomy everywhere, here's how to plug your computer into your hobby: use the machine to discover distances across the Universe!

This program converts lightyears to kilometers or kilometers to lightyears or lightyears to miles or miles to lightyears. It's hard to visualize distances in lightyears. Run this program and you'll be better able to grasp the vast expanse of the Cosmos with your mind.

Of course, all distances are approximate. We use 365.86 days per year and, thus, 9.4830912×10^{12}km/ly or $5.892792872 \times 10^{12}$mi/ly.

Program Listing

```
10 PRINT "}":REM CLEAR SCREEN
20 DIM K$(1)
30 PRINT :PRINT
40 FOR L=1 TO 30:PRINT "+";:NEXT L
50 PRINT
60 PRINT "LIGHTYEARS DISTANCE CONVERSION"
70 FOR L=1 TO 30:PRINT "+";:NEXT L
80 PRINT :PRINT
100 PRINT "YOUR CHOICES ARE:"
110 PRINT "(1)  LIGHTYEARS TO KILOMETERS"
120 PRINT "(2)  LIGHTYEARS TO MILES"
130 PRINT "(3)  KILOMETERS TO LIGHTYEARS"
140 PRINT "(4)  MILES TO LIGHTYEARS"
150 PRINT :PRINT "WHICH CONVERSION: ";
160 INPUT C
170 IF C<1 OR C>4 THEN 80
180 IF C>2 THEN 400
```

```
200 PRINT "}":REM BUZZER
210 PRINT "LIGHTYEARS: ";
220 INPUT L
230 K=L*(9.4830912*(10^12))
240 M=L*(5.89279287*(10^12))
250 IF C=2 THEN 320
260 PRINT
270 PRINT "KILOMETERS = ";K
280 PRINT :PRINT
290 PRINT "FOR MORE, PRESS RETURN"
300 INPUT K$
310 CLR :GOTO 10
320 PRINT
330 PRINT "MILES = ";M
340 GOTO 280
400 PRINT "}":REM BUZZER
410 IF C=4 THEN 480
420 PRINT "KILOMETERS: ";
430 INPUT K
440 L=K/(9.4830912*(10^12))
450 PRINT
460 PRINT "LIGHTYEARS = ";L
470 GOTO 280
480 PRINT "MILES: ";
490 INPUT M
500 L=M/(5.89279287*(10^12))
510 GOTO 450
```

State Geographic Centers

This mind bender tests your knowledge of geographic locations of cities and towns in the United States. These are special places since, in each case, they are the town nearest to the geographic center of its state.

In other words, Columbus happens to be almost exactly in the center of Ohio. But which state has Challis at its center? Or Lewistown? Or Oklahoma City? (Well, some may be obvious!)

You not only learn a lot from running this program but you have a barrel of fun. Talk about trivia!

Program Listing

```
10 PRINT "}":REM CLEAR SCREEN
15 DIM S$(20),C$(20),D$(20)
20 DATA CLANTON,ALABAMA
30 DATA MT. MCKINLEY,ALASKA
40 DATA PRESCOTT,ARIZONA
50 DATA LITTLE ROCK,ARKANSAS
60 DATA MADERA,CALIFORNIA
70 DATA PIKES PEAK,COLORADO
80 DATA EAST BERLIN,CONNECTICUT
90 DATA DOVER,DELAWARE
100 DATA BROOKSVILLE,FLORIDA
110 DATA MACON,GEORGIA
120 DATA MAUI ISLAND,HAWAII
130 DATA CHALLIS,IDAHO
140 DATA SPRINGFIELD,ILLINOIS
150 DATA INDIANAPOLIS,INDIANA
160 DATA AMES,IOWA
170 DATA GREAT BANK,KANSAS
180 DATA LEBANON,KENTUCKY
190 DATA MARKSVILLE,LOUISIANA
200 DATA DOVER-FOXCROFT,MAINE
210 DATA DAVIDSONVILLE,MARYLAND
220 DATA WORCESTER,MASSACHUSETTS
230 DATA CADILLAC,MICHIGAN
240 DATA BRAINERD,MINNESOTA
250 DATA CARTHAGE,MISSISSIPPI
260 DATA JEFFERSON CITY,MISSOURI
270 DATA LEWISTOWN,MONTANA
280 DATA BROKEN BOW,NEBRASKA
290 DATA AUSTIN,NEVADA
300 DATA ASHLAND,NEW HAMPSHIRE
310 DATA TRENTON,NEW JERSEY
320 DATA WILLARD,NEW MEXICO
330 DATA ONEIDA,NEW YORK
340 DATA SANFORD,NORTH CAROLINA
```

```
350 DATA MCCLUSKY,NORTH DAKOTA
360 DATA COLUMBUS,OHIO
370 DATA OKLAHOMA CITY,OKLAHOMA
380 DATA PRINEVILLE,OREGON
390 DATA BELLEFONTE,PENNSYLVANIA
400 DATA CROMPTON,RHODE ISLAND
410 DATA COLUMBIA,SOUTH CAROLINA
420 DATA PIERRE,SOUTH DAKOTA
430 DATA MURFREESBORO,TENNESSEE
440 DATA BRADY,TEXAS
450 DATA MANTI,UTAH
460 DATA ROXBURY,VERMONT
470 DATA BUCKINGHAM,VIRGINIA
480 DATA WENATCHEE,WASHINGTON
490 DATA SUTTON,WEST VIRGINIA
500 DATA MARSHFIELD,WISCONSIN
510 DATA LANDER,WYOMING
520 PRINT "FOR HOW MANY STATES"
530 PRINT "CAN YOU NAME"
535 PRINT "THE GEOGRAPHICAL CENTER ?"
540 R=INT(100*(RND(1)))
550 IF R<1 THEN 540
560 IF INT(R/2)=R/2 THEN R=R-1
570 FOR L=1 TO R
580 READ S$
590 NEXT L
600 PRINT :PRINT
610 PRINT "WHICH STATE HAS ITS"
620 PRINT "GEOGRAPHIC CENTER NEAR"
630 PRINT S$
640 READ C$
650 INPUT D$
660 PRINT
670 IF C$=D$ THEN PRINT "RIGHT":GOTO 690
680 PRINT "WRONG"
690 PRINT "THE CENTER OF ";C$
695 PRINT "IS ";S$
700 RESTORE
710 PRINT :PRINT
720 GOTO 540
```

Volumes

Cones. Cubes. Cylinders. Prisms. Pyramids. Spheres. Name your object. This program computes the volume and displays it in cubic units.

Put in inches, get cubic inches. Put in feet, get cubic feet. Yards, get cubic yards. No mixing units in any one calculation. Cylinder is right circular.

Program Listing

```
10 PRINT "}":REM CLEAR SCREEN
20 DIM X$(10)
30 PRINT "OBJECT: ";
40 INPUT X$
50 PRINT
60 IF X$="CONE" THEN 100
65 IF X$="CUBE" THEN 200
70 IF X$="CYLINDER" THEN 300
75 IF X$="PRISM" THEN 400
80 IF X$="PYRAMID" THEN 100
85 IF X$="SPHERE" THEN 500
90 IF X$="PRISM" THEN 400
95 PRINT :GOTO 30
100 PRINT "AREA = ";
110 INPUT A
120 PRINT "HEIGHTH = ";
130 INPUT H
140 V=(A*H)/3
150 GOTO 600
200 PRINT "LENGTH = ";
210 INPUT L
220 PRINT "WIDTH = ";
230 INPUT W
240 PRINT "HEIGHTH = ";
250 INPUT H
260 V=L*W*H
270 GOTO 600
300 PRINT "RADIUS = ";
310 INPUT R
320 PRINT "HEIGHTH = ";
```

```
330 INPUT H
340 V=3.14*2*R*H
350 GOTO 600
400 PRINT "AREA = ";
410 INPUT A
420 PRINT "HEIGHTH = ";
430 INPUT H
440 V=A*H
450 GOTO 600
500 PRINT "RADIUS = ";
510 INPUT R
520 V=(3.14*4*(R^3))/3
600 PRINT
610 PRINT "VOLUME = ";V
620 PRINT :GOTO 30
```

Sample Run

```
OBJECT:
PRISM
AREA =
71
HEIGHTH =
18
VOLUME = 1278

OBJECT:
CUBE
LENGTH =
13
WIDTH =
8
HEIGHTH =
24
VOLUME = 2496

CONE
AREA =
55
HEIGHTH =
66
VOLUME = 1210
```

Event Timer

Place your computer in a corner and let it time your next chess match. Three-minute egg. Final exam.

The computer asks how many minutes you want for the event you are timing, and then it sounds a bell when the time has passed.

You can calibrate the clock by changing the value of SP in line 10. A larger number will slow down the clock. A smaller value for SP will speed up the clock. As you can see we have started with an SP value of 8.

If you want to time an event of less than one minute, use a decimal. For instance, when you want to time a 30-second event, respond to the computer's inquiry with .5 or for 45 seconds key in .75. Use .17 for 10 seconds; .25 for 15 seconds.

Program Listing

```
10 SP=8:DIM S$(1),T$(1)
20 PRINT "}":REM CLEAR SCREEN
30 PRINT "EVENT TIMER":PRINT
40 PRINT "HOW MANY MINUTES"
50 PRINT "TO THE END OF THE EVENT"
60 INPUT LT
70 PRINT
80 PRINT "TO START TIMING, PRESS RETURN"
90 INPUT S$
100 PRINT "}":REM CLEAR SCREEN
110 C=C+1
120 IF C>(SP*LT*60) THEN 300
130 MN=INT(C/SP/60)
140 SC=INT((C/SP)-(60*MN))
150 PRINT MN;" MINUTES ";SC;" SECONDS"
160 GOTO 110
300 PRINT "}":REM CLEAR SCREEN
310 PRINT "}":REM BUZZER
320 PRINT "TIME IS UP"
330 PRINT LT;" MINUTES HAVE PASSED"
340 FOR L=1 TO 10:PRINT :NEXT L
350 PRINT "TO TIME AGAIN, PRESS RETURN"
360 INPUT T$
370 CLR :GOTO 10
```

Programs for the business person

Profit Estimator

How much cash flow will I generate if I sell 100 thingamabobs? A question faced everyday in the business office. Whether you sell large lots at wholesale, small quantities across the retail counter, or individual items via mail order, this program will give you a quick estimate of expected cash flow and potential profits. It allows fast comparisons when quick decisions are needed.

The computer asks you questions about the quantity of items involved, prices, quantity sold, discounts, etc. Then it calculates unit price, unit profit, gross profit, return percentages, sales needed to break even, and more, depending upon which part of the program you are using.

The program is divided into four main blocks:

—an opening billboard from line 10 through line 210;
—wholesale computations, lines 1000 to 1320;
—mail order computations, lines 2000 to 2360;
—ad response computations, lines 3000 to 3590.

Remember that the program only *estimates*, it is not exact. The wholesale, direct-mail, or ad-response manufacturing cost asked by the computer is *total*, not per unit.

This program is a useful tool for small business, whether a local furniture store, supermarket, wholesaler, or regional mail-order house.

Program Listing

```
10 PRINT "}":DIM Q$(1)
20 PRINT "PROFIT ESTIMATOR"
30 PRINT
40 PRINT "WHICH TYPE OF SALE:"
50 PRINT "WHOLESALE (W)"
60 PRINT "DIRECT MAIL (D)"
70 PRINT "MEDIA AD RESPONSE (M)"
80 PRINT
100 PRINT "}"
110 PRINT "W, D OR M ?"
120 INPUT Q$
130 IF Q$="W" THEN 1000
```

```
140 IF Q$="D" THEN 2000
150 IF Q$="M" THEN 3000
160 PRINT "OKAY, YOU SELECTED ";Q$
170 PRINT "HOWEVER, ";Q$;" IS NOT"
180 PRINT "A CHOICE.  TRY AGAIN."
200 PRINT
210 GOTO 100
1000 PRINT "}":CLR :DIM A$(1)
1010 PRINT "WHOLESALE"
1020 PRINT "PROFIT ESTIMATOR"
1030 PRINT
1040 PRINT "}"
1060 PRINT "PLEASE ANSWER THESE QUESTIONS"
1070 PRINT :PRINT "MANUFACTURING COST $"
1080 INPUT C
1090 PRINT "}":PRINT "QUANTITY MANUFACTURED"
1100 INPUT P
1110 PRINT "}":PRINT "LIST PRICE OF ITEM $"
1120 INPUT L
1130 PRINT "}":PRINT "TOTAL QUANTITY SOLD"
1140 INPUT S
1150 IF S<>0 THEN 1160
1155 GOTO 10
1160 PRINT "WHOLESALE DISCOUNT %"
1165 INPUT D
1170 UC=C/P
1180 UP=(L*((100-D)/100))-UC
1190 W=L*S*((100-D)/100)
1200 G=W-(S*UC)
1210 PRINT "}"
1220 PRINT
1230 PRINT "------"
1240 PRINT "UNIT COST IS $";UC
1250 PRINT "UNIT PROFIT IS $";UP
1260 PRINT "WHOLESALE GROSS $";W
1270 PRINT "WHOLESALE PROFIT $";G
1280 PRINT "------"
1290 PRINT
1300 PRINT "FOR MORE, PRESS M AND RETURN"
1310 PRINT
1320 INPUT A$
1330 IF A$="M" THEN 10
```

```
1340 PRINT "THANK YOU."
1350 END
2000 PRINT "}":CLR :DIM A$(1)
2010 PRINT "DIRECT MAIL"
2020 PRINT "PROFIT ESTIMATOR"
2030 PRINT
2050 PRINT "}"
2060 PRINT "PLEASE ANSWER THESE QUESTIONS"
2070 PRINT :PRINT "MANUFACTURING COST $"
2080 INPUT C
2090 PRINT "}":PRINT "QUANTITY MANUFACTURED"
2100 INPUT P
2110 PRINT "}":PRINT "LIST PRICE OF ITEM $"
2120 INPUT L
2130 PRINT "}":PRINT "TOTAL QUANTITY SOLD"
2140 INPUT S
2150 PRINT "}":PRINT "NUMBER FLYERS MAILED ?"
2160 INPUT K
2170 PRINT "}":PRINT "FLYER PRINTING COST $"
2180 INPUT R
2190 PRINT "}":PRINT "POSTAGE COST $"
2200 INPUT M
2210 UC=C/P
2220 J=100*S/K
2230 T=L*S-(R+M+UC*S)
2240 U=L*S
2250 PRINT "}"
2260 PRINT
2270 PRINT "--------"
2280 PRINT "DIRECT MAIL"
2290 PRINT "RETURN IS ";J;" PERCENT"
2300 PRINT "DIRECT MAIL GROSS $";U
2310 PRINT "DIRECT MAIL PROFIT $";T
2320 PRINT "--------"
2330 PRINT
2340 PRINT "FOR MORE, PRESS M AND RETURN"
2350 PRINT
2360 INPUT A$
2370 IF A$="M" THEN 10
2380 PRINT "THANK YOU"
2390 END
3000 PRINT "}":CLR :DIM A$(1)
```

```
3010 PRINT "RESPONSE TO ADVERTISEMENT"
3020 PRINT "PROFIT ESTIMATOR"
3030 PRINT
3050 PRINT "}"
3060 PRINT "PLEASE ANSWER THESE QUESTIONS"
3070 PRINT :PRINT "MANUFACTURING COST $"
3080 INPUT C
3090 PRINT "}":PRINT "QUANTITY MANUFACTURED"
3100 INPUT P
3110 PRINT "}":PRINT "LIST PRICE OF ITEM $"
3120 INPUT L
3130 PRINT "}":PRINT "AD COST PER INSERTION $"
3140 INPUT A
3150 PRINT "}":PRINT "NUMBER OF INSERTIONS ?"
3160 INPUT I
3170 PRINT "}"
3180 PRINT "}"
3190 PRINT "WHICH DO YOU WANT TO KNOW ?"
3200 PRINT
3210 PRINT "SALES QUANTITY NEEDED"
3220 PRINT "TO BREAK EVEN (Q)"
3230 PRINT
3240 PRINT "PROFIT FROM SELLING"
3250 PRINT "A SPECIFIC QUANTITY (P)"
3260 PRINT
3270 PRINT "P OR Q ?"
3280 INPUT A$
3290 IF A$="P" THEN 3460
3300 IF A$="Q" THEN 3330
3310 GOTO 3270
3320 PRINT
3330 PRINT
3340 B=INT((C+A)/L)+1
3350 PRINT "--------"
3360 PRINT "SELL ";B;" TO BREAK EVEN"
3370 PRINT "INCLUDING COVERING"
3380 PRINT "$";C;" MANUFACTURING COST"
3390 PRINT "AND $";A*I;" AD CAMPAIGN"
3400 PRINT "--------"
3410 PRINT
3420 PRINT "FOR MORE, PRESS M AND RETURN"
3430 INPUT A$
```

```
3440 IF A$="M" THEN 10
3450 PRINT "THANK YOU":END
3460 PRINT :PRINT "QUANTITY SOLD ?"
3470 INPUT S
3480 N=S*L
3490 UC=C/P
3500 E=S*L-S*UC-A*I
3510 PRINT
3520 PRINT "--------"
3530 PRINT "ORDERS GROSS IS $";N
3540 PRINT "DIRECT MAIL PROFIT IS $";E
3550 PRINT "--------"
3560 PRINT
3570 PRINT "FOR MORE, PRESS M AND RETURN"
3580 INPUT A$
3590 IF A$="M" THEN 10
3600 PRINT "THANK YOU"
3610 END
```

Daily Codes

Businesses everywhere are concerned about security. Banks, credit card managers, warehousemen, shipping clerks, office managers, all need private daily codes for internal use to prevent unauthorized admission to storage areas, financial records, private files.

Now you can use your own computer to generate a set of secret codes, one for each day of the week. This program generates a series of pseudorandom numbers and displays a table of those numbers alongside names of the days of the week.

The subroutine in lines 200 to 220 generates four-digit random numbers.

Program Listing

```
10 PRINT "}":DIM KY$(1)
20 GOSUB 200
30 PRINT "SUNDAY:      ";C:GOSUB 200
```

```
40 PRINT "MONDAY:        ";C:GOSUB 200
50 PRINT "TUESDAY:       ";C:GOSUB 200
60 PRINT "WEDNESDAY:     ";C:GOSUB 200
70 PRINT "THURSDAY:      ";C:GOSUB 200
80 PRINT "FRIDAY:        ";C:GOSUB 200
90 PRINT "SATURDAY:      ";C
100 PRINT :PRINT
110 PRINT "FOR A NEW SET OF NUMBERS"
120 PRINT "PRESS RETURN KEY"
130 INPUT KY$
140 CLR :GOTO 10
200 C=INT(10000*(RND(1)))
210 IF C<1000 THEN 200
220 RETURN
```

Invoice Computer

The computer will ask you for a discount percentage to be applied to the invoice; the retail price of goods being invoiced; and the quantity of those goods.

You enter actual percentage. The computer changes that to the appropriate decimal vaue.

Then it will ask if you have other items to be shown on the same invoice. If so, it again will get price and quantity sold info from you. It will assume the same discount applies.

When you tell the computer there are no more items for the same invoice, it will compute and display the total.

Program Listing

```
10 DIM IT$(9),Z$(1):GOSUB 600
20 PRINT "INFO FOR COMPUTING INVOICES:"
30 PRINT "DISCOUNT PERCENT % ":INPUT DP
40 DD=1-0.01*DP
50 PRINT "THE ITEM SOLD:":INPUT IT$
60 PRINT "RETAIL PRICE $ ":INPUT P
70 PRINT "QUANTITY SOLD:":INPUT Q
80 C=P*DD:I=C*Q:T=T+I
```

```
90 PRINT :PRINT "WHOLESALE COST"
100 PRINT "OF ";Q;" ";IT$;"S: ";I
110 PRINT :PRINT "MORE SAME INVOICE?"
120 PRINT "PRESS M AND RETURN"
130 PRINT "IF NONE, PRESS E AND RETURN"
140 INPUT Z$
150 PRINT :IF Z$="M" THEN 50
160 IF Z$="E" THEN 200
170 GOTO 110
200 PRINT "}"
210 PRINT "INVOICE GRAND TOTAL: $";T
220 PRINT :PRINT "TO DO OTHER INVOICES"
230 PRINT "AT OTHER DISCOUNTS,"
240 PRINT "PRESS M AND RETURN"
250 PRINT "TO QUIT, PRESS Q AND RETURN"
260 INPUT Z$
270 PRINT :IF Z$="M" THEN CLR :GOTO 10
280 IF Z$="Q" THEN END
290 GOTO 220
300 END
600 PRINT "}"
610 PRINT "**********************"
620 PRINT "* INVOICE COMPUTER *"
630 PRINT "**********************"
640 RETURN
```

Hourly Wages

This handy program computes total hours worked at regular pay and number of hours worked at time-and-a-half overtime. It then finds gross pay and rounds off to the nearest cent. The program knows that overtime starts after 40 hours.

The result is a nice chart on the display, after the computer asks only three questions.

You can change the number of regular-work hours per week by changing the number 40 in lines 200 and 210. Change the overtime multiplier of 1.5 by changing the number 1.5 in line 300.

This program makes payroll booking quick and simple.

Program Listing

```
10 PRINT "}":REM SCREEN CLEAR
15 PRINT "}":REM BUZZER
20 PRINT :PRINT :DIM N$(20),KY$(1)
30 PRINT "****************"
40 PRINT "* HOURLY WAGES *"
50 PRINT "****************"
60 PRINT :PRINT
100 PRINT "EMPLOYEE'S NAME: ":INPUT N$
110 PRINT "}":REM BUZZER
120 PRINT "HOURLY PAY RATE $":INPUT P
130 PRINT "}":REM BUZZER
140 PRINT "TOTAL HOURS WORKED: ":INPUT H
150 PRINT "}":REM BUZZER
200 IF H<40.001 THEN RH=H:OH=0:GOTO 300
210 IF H>40 THEN OH=H-40:RH=40
300 OP=1.5*P:PA=RH*P:PB=OH*OP
310 PY=PA+PB
320 PY=INT(100*PY+0.5)/100
400 PRINT "}":REM SCREEN
410 PRINT "EMPLOYEE: ";N$
420 PRINT
430 PRINT "TOTAL HOURS: ";H
440 PRINT
450 PRINT "REGULAR HOURS: ";RH
460 PRINT "REGULAR RATE $";P
470 PRINT "TOTAL REGULAR DOLLARS $";PA
480 PRINT
490 PRINT "OVERTIME HOURS: ";OH
500 PRINT "OVERTIME RATE $";OP
510 PRINT "TOTAL OVERTIME $";PB
520 PRINT
530 PRINT "GROSS PAY $";PY
600 FOR L=1 TO 5:PRINT :NEXT L
610 PRINT "TO COMPUTE WAGES FOR A"
620 PRINT "DIFFERENT EMPLOYEE,"
630 PRINT "PRESS RETURN"
640 INPUT KY$
650 CLR :GOTO 10
```

Sample Run

```
*****************
* HOURLY WAGES *
*****************

EMPLOYEE'S NAME:
JONES          RETURN
HOURLY PAY RATE:
5.00           RETURN
TOTAL NUMBER OF HOURS WORKED:
50             RETURN


EMPLOYEE:  JONES

TOTAL HOURS:      50

REGULAR HOURS:    40
REGULAR RATE:     $5
TOTAL REGULAR:    $200

OVERTIME HOURS:   10
OVERTIME RATE:    $7.5
TOTAL OVERTIME:   $75

GROSS PAY:        $2.75
```

Ad Campaign Profit

The ad salesman is standing in your office pressing for your answer. Do you want to advertise or not? Advertising costs plenty of money today. How can you make a quick decision about whether or not sales from advertising would be worth the cost?

In this program, the computer asks you for information about the list price of the item you would sell through advertising. It asks for the manufacturing cost of that item; the cost of the advertising campaign; and the number of units sold.

It computes your gross sales and deducts the cost of manufacturing and advertising to show an estimate of profits to be expected. If you key in a zero in response to the number-sold question, the machine will inquire as to the amount of profit you would like to make and then tell you how many units you would have to sell to make such a profit.

If you would like to make your own changes to this program listing, you'll want to know that memory location B holds the list price of the item you are selling; C is the unit manufacturing cost of the item; D is the total advertising cost; A is the number of units sold of the item; E is the profit on the sales of the item; and F is the profit you say you want to make.

Suppose you have an item you sell for $9.95 and it costs you $1.25 to produce it. An ad campaign costing $330 results in sales of 50 units. Your profit from the campaign would be $105. If you only wanted to know how many units you would have to sell to break even, enter zero in response to the number-sold question and $1 to the profit-wanted question. You'll discover you need to sell just over 38 units to break even.

Program Listing

```
10 PRINT "}":REM CLEAR SCREEN
20 CLR
30 PRINT "LIST $"
40 INPUT B
50 PRINT "MANUFACTURING COST $"
60 INPUT C
70 PRINT "ADVERTISING COST $"
80 INPUT D
90 PRINT "QUANTITY SOLD"
100 INPUT A
110 IF A=0 THEN 200
120 E=A*B-A*C-D
130 PRINT :PRINT
140 PRINT "PROFIT:","$";E
```

```
150 PRINT :PRINT
160 GOTO 90
200 PRINT "PROFIT WANTED $"
210 INPUT F
220 A=(F+D)/(B-C)
230 PRINT :PRINT
240 PRINT "SELL:",A
250 PRINT "PROFIT:","$";F
260 PRINT :PRINT
270 GOTO 90
```

Media Money Massage

If you have used the *Ad Campaign Profit* program earlier in this book, you know how many bucks you can expect to make from advertising. But, suppose two salesmen are standing in your office. One from your local newspaper and the other from a local television station. Both want your advertising dollar and you can't decide which is the best buy.

This program compares the cost of advertising in two media and reports which is most favorable. First it computes cost-per-thousand. Then it highlights the least-expensive medium.

And, it compares any media—newspaper, radio, television, magazines, shoppers, etc.

Imagine your friendly salesmen are from the Daily Post and the Evening News. The ad in the Post costs $250. In the News it is $300. The Post's circulation is 27,500 readers. The News has 32,500 readers. Which is the better buy? The Post is about 14¢ cheaper per thousand readers.

Program Listing

```
10 PRINT "}":REM CLEAR SCREEN
20 DIM N$(20),P$(20),K$(1)
30 PRINT "FIRST MEDIUM: "
```

```
40 INPUT N$
50 PRINT "ADVERTISING COST $"
60 INPUT A
70 PRINT "CIRCULATION:"
80 INPUT C
90 M=1000*(A/C)
100 PRINT
110 PRINT "SECOND MEDIUM:"
120 INPUT P$
130 PRINT "ADVERTISING COST $"
140 INPUT Q
150 PRINT "CIRCULATION:"
160 INPUT R
170 S=1000*(Q/R)
200 PRINT "}":REM CLEAR SCREEN
210 PRINT "}":REM BUZZER
220 PRINT :PRINT
230 FOR L=1 TO 23:PRINT "*";:NEXT L
240 PRINT
250 IF S>M THEN 300
260 IF M>S THEN 400
300 PRINT N$
310 PRINT "HAS A LOWER"
320 PRINT "COST PER THOUSAND"
330 PRINT "AT $";M
340 GOTO 500
400 PRINT P$
410 PRINT "HAS A LOWER"
420 PRINT "COST PER THOUSAND"
430 PRINT "AT $";S
500 PRINT
510 PRINT N$
520 PRINT "COST PER THOUSAND: $";M
530 PRINT "ADVERTISING COST: $";A
540 PRINT "CIRCULATION: ";C
550 PRINT
560 PRINT P$
570 PRINT "COST PER THOUSAND: $";S
580 PRINT "ADVERTISING COST: $";Q
590 PRINT "CIRCULATION: ";R
600 FOR L=1 TO 23:PRINT "*";:NEXT L
700 PRINT :PRINT
```

```
710 PRINT "FOR MORE, PRESS RETURN"
720 INPUT K$
730 CLR :GOTO 10
```

Sales Required For A Profit

This handy program gives a quick estimate of how many units have to be sold, at a certain "profit" or cashflow amount per unit, to achieve a desired gross profit or cashflow.

Suppose you sell Widgets. Each Widget sold provides a profit of $5. You decide you want an income of $30,000 from selling these Widgets. How many Widgets must you sell? Per year? Per month? Per week? Per day?

By the way, this program assumes a six-day workweek. If you want to use a five-day workweek, change the number 6 at the end of line 70 to 5.

Very handy!

Program Listing

```
10 PRINT "}":REM CLEAR SCREEN
20 DIM X$(1)
30 PRINT "INCOME WANTED = $"
40 INPUT I
50 PRINT "PROFIT/UNIT SOLD = $"
60 INPUT P
70 Y=I/P:M=Y/12:W=Y/52:D=W/6
100 PRINT :PRINT
110 PRINT "SELL ";Y;" PER YR"
120 PRINT "SELL ";M;" PER MO"
130 PRINT "SELL ";W;" PER WEEK"
140 PRINT "SELL ";D;" PER DAY"
200 PRINT :PRINT :PRINT
210 PRINT "TO DO MORE, PRESS RETURN"
220 INPUT X$
230 CLR :GOTO 10
```

Sample Run

```
INCOME WANTED = $
30000
PROFIT/UNIT SOLD = $
5

SELL 6000 PER YR
SELL 500 PER MO
SELL 115.384615 PER WEEK
SELL 19.23076916 PER DAY
```

Salesman's Commission

Representatives, salesmen, account representatives, sales representatives. Here's the no-sweat way to compute commissions to be paid to your sales corps.

The computer will ask you for pertinent data and then display results including the salesman's name, the pay period, his commission percentage rate, gross sales, and commission payable.

Program Listing

```
10 DIM D$(20),N$(20),KY$(1)
15 PRINT "}":REM CLEAR SCREEN
20 PRINT "}":REM BUZZER
25 PRINT ">>>>> REP COMMISSIONS <<<<<"
30 PRINT
35 PRINT
40 PRINT "SALES PERIOD ENDING DATE"
45 INPUT D$
50 PRINT "SALESMAN'S NAME: "
55 INPUT N$
60 PRINT "COMMISSION PERCENTAGE %"
65 INPUT P
70 K=P*0.01
```

```
80 PRINT "SALESMAN'S GROSS SALES $"
85 INPUT Q
90 T=K*Q
95 PRINT "}":REM CLEAR SCREEN
100 PRINT "}":REM BUZZER
110 PRINT "SALESMAN: ";N$
120 PRINT "PERIOD ENDING: ";D$
130 PRINT "COMMISSION RATE: ";P;"%"
140 PRINT "GROSS SALES: $";Q
150 PRINT "COMMISSION: $";T
160 FOR L=1 TO 8:PRINT :NEXT L
170 PRINT "FOR ANOTHER,"
180 PRINT "PRESS ANY RETURN"
190 INPUT KY$
200 CLR :GOTO 10
```

Sample Run

```
REP COMMISSIONS

SALES PERIOD ENDING DATE:
12/31/83            RETURN

SALESMAN'S NAME:
SMITH               RETURN

COMMISSION PERCENTAGE:
15                  RETURN

SALESMAN'S GROSS SALES: $
16243.00            RETURN


SALESMAN:           SMITH
PERIOD ENDING:      12/31/83
COMMISSION RATE:    15%
GROSS SALES:        $16243
COMMISSION:         $2436.45
```

Unit Price

Suppose you find 895 green Widgets and buy them for $695. How much did each green Widget cost? Rounded off, $7.77.

Unit price is total price divided by quantity. The quantity can be expressed in weight, total numbers, etc. It works the same whether you are talking about pounds of coffee, yards of concrete, gallons of ice cream, boxes of books, or units of Widgets.

This program asks for the name of the item, quantity purchased and total price paid. It then displays quantity, name, total and unit price.

Program Listing

```
10 DIM N$(20),KY$(1)
20 PRINT "}":REM CLEAR SCREEN
30 PRINT "***************"
40 PRINT "* UNIT PRICE *"
50 PRINT "***************"
60 PRINT :PRINT
70 PRINT "NAME OF ITEM: "
80 INPUT N$
90 PRINT "QUANTITY OF ITEMS: "
100 INPUT Q
110 PRINT "TOTAL PRICE FOR ALL ITEMS $"
120 INPUT P
130 U=P/Q
140 PRINT "}":REM BUZZER
150 PRINT
160 PRINT
170 PRINT Q;" ";N$;"S";" TOTAL $";P
180 PRINT "EACH ";N$;" IS $";U
190 FOR L=1 TO 8:PRINT :NEXT L
200 PRINT "TO DO MORE, PRESS RETURN"
210 INPUT KY$
220 CLR :GOTO 10
```

Sample Run

```
UNIT PRICE

NAME OF ITEM
WIDGET   RETURN

QUANTITY OF ITEMS
150      RETURN

TOTAL PRICE FOR ALL ITEMS $
88.75    RETURN


150 WIDGETS TOTAL $88.75
EACH WIDGET $.59166666
```

Gross & Net Computer

How much cash flow will I generate if I sell 100 thingamabobs? A question faced everyday in the business office. Whether you sell large lots at wholesale, small quantities across the retail counter, or individual items via mail order, this program will give you a quick estimate of expected cash flow and potential profits.

It allows fast comparisons when quick decisions are needed. The computer asks you questions and then generates the answers you need in an attractive chart.

In response to its inquiries on the display, tell the computer how much it costs to manufacture your thingamabob, what its list price is and at what discount you plan to sell the thingamabobs. As soon as you tell the computer how many thingamabobs you will sell, it will compute the total invoice amount you will charge your customer and your anticipated profits after manufacturing costs are deducted.

This program is a useful tool for small business,

whether a local furniture store, supermarket or regional mail-order house.

Program Listing

```
10 DIM T$(20),K$(1)
20 PRINT "}":REM CLEAR SCREEN
30 PRINT "ITEM:"
40 INPUT T$
50 PRINT "LIST PRICE $"
60 INPUT L
70 PRINT "MANUFACTURING COST $"
80 INPUT C
90 PRINT "WHOLESALE DISCOUNT %"
100 INPUT W
110 D=1-0.01*W
120 PRINT "QUANTITY SOLD"
130 INPUT S
140 I=L*S*D:P=I-S*C
200 PRINT "}":REM CLEAR SCREEN
210 PRINT "ITEM:",,T$
220 PRINT "LIST PRICE","$";L
230 PRINT "MFG COST",,"$";C
240 PRINT "SOLD",,S
250 PRINT "DISCOUNT",,W;"%"
260 PRINT
270 PRINT "INVOICE",,"$";I
280 PRINT "PROFIT",,"$";P
300 PRINT :PRINT :PRINT :PRINT
310 PRINT "FOR MORE, PRESS RETURN"
320 INPUT K$
330 CLR :GOTO 10
```

Sample Run

```
ITEM: WIDGET
LIST PRICE $9.95
MFG COST $1.35
SOLD 500
DISCOUNT 50.%
```

```
INVOICE $2487.5
PROFIT $1812.5


ITEM: THINGAMAGIG
LIST PRICE $5.95
MFG COST $0.95
SOLD 500
DISCOUNT 50.%
INVOICE $1487.5
PROFIT $1012.5
```

Executive Decision Maker

Stumped by a toughie? Got one too hot to handle alone? Need help with major decisions? When there is no other way to decide, punch up this quickie and get a definite YES or NO.

Program Listing

```
10 DIM KY$(1)
20 PRINT "}":REM CLEAR SCREEN
30 R=INT(1000*(RND(1)))
40 IF R>499 THEN PRINT "YES":GOTO 60
50 PRINT "NO"
60 FOR L=1 TO 10:PRINT :NEXT L
70 PRINT "TO MAKE ANOTHER"
80 PRINT "IMPORTANT DECISION,"
90 PRINT "PRESS RETURN"
100 INPUT KY$
110 PRINT "}":REM BUZZER
120 CLR
130 GOTO 10
```

Appendix

Appendix A: ATARI BASIC Words

Here is a handy list of all the words in the ATARI version of the BASIC computer language:

ABS	absolute value function
ADR	string memory address function
AND	logical expression true only if both are
ASC	finds ASCII character number
ATN	arctangent
BYE	leave BASIC; write directly on screen
CLOAD	load program from tape
CHR$	converts ASCII number to character
CLOG	base 10 logarithm
CLOSE	close file at end of I/O job
CLR	undimensions strings and arrays
COLOR	select color register for graphics
COM	same as DIM
CONT	continue, after BREAK or STOP
COS	cosine
CSAVE	sends data from computer to tape

DATA	stores info in program line
DEG	switch to trig degrees from radians
DIM	reserves memory for array or string
DOS	displays disk menu
DRAWTO	draws line between points
END	concludes a program run
ENTER	input data or programs
EXP	e to a power
FOR	sets range of FOR/NEXT loop
FRE	shows remaining available memory
GET	input single byte of data, with disk
GOSUB	branch to subroutine
GOTO	branch to a line
GRAPHICS	selects graphics mode
IF	decision maker
INPUT	stops for keyboard input of data
INT	portion of number left of decimal
LEN	number of characters in a string
LET	optional; assigns value to variable
LIST	display contents of program memory
LOAD	send program from disk to computer
LOCATE	stores specific graphics point
LOG	natural logarithm
LPRINT	print on paper with line printer
NEW	erase all program and data memory
NEXT	other half of FOR/NEXT loop
NOT	not true =1; true =0
NOTE	used with disk
ON	use with GOTO or GOSUB branches
OPEN	opens a file for I/O
OR	if either true, a 1; 0 if both false
PADDLE	position of game paddle
PEEK	look in one memory location
PLOT	light a single dot on video screen
POINT	for disk operations
POKE	put info in one memory location
POP	abnormal departure from GOSUB loop
POSITION	move to specific video screen point
PRINT	causes output from the computer
PTRIG	status of trigger button on paddle
PUT	output one data byte from computer
RAD	trig info in rads, not degrees

READ	get info from DATA lines
REM	ignore these remarks
RESTORE	allows DATA lines to be re-read
RETURN	back from subroutine to main program
RND	random number between 0 and 1
RUN	execute a program
SAVE	store data or program on disk
SETCOLOR	store color data
SGN	find sign of a number
SIN	sine
SOUND	control pitch, volume, tone
SQR	square root
STATUS	asks state of I/O device
STEP	size of skip in FOR/NEXT loop
STICK	position of stick game controller
STRIG	determines if stick trigger button is pressed
STOP	temporary program run halt
STR$	changes number to character string
THEN	IF true, does what follows
TO	part of FOR/NEXT loop range
TRAP	on input error, jumps to a line
USR	machine-language subroutine
VAL	converts string to a number
XIO	I/O in graphics or disk work

Appendix B: Error Messages

These are the messages your ATARI is trying to send you when it presents an error number. Naturally, it tells you the line number where the error is located.

Number	Message
2	you have used up all available memory
3	the number can't have the value it has
4	you are only allowed 128 different variable names
5	your string is longer than the space you dimensioned
6	you are tryng to READ more DATA than you have available
7	a number is greater than 32767
8	you are trying to put string data in a number variable
9	you have not dimensioned an array or string properly
10	you simply have too many GOSUBs
11	you either have tried to divide by zero or else you want a result too large or too small for the computer to handle

12	you are using GOSUB or GOTO or THEN to jump to a nonexistent line number
13	you have a NEXT but there was no FOR
14	the statement simply is too long or too complex for BASIC to handle
15	again you have tried a NEXT or a RETURN without the necessary FOR or GOSUB
16	there is a RETURN without a GOSUB
17	don't POKE there; try NEW to get out of this mess; if that doesn't work, kill the power and turn it back on and re-enter the program without POKEs
18	you are trying to use an invalid string character
19	there's not enough memory to complete the LOAD
20	you have a device number larger than 7 or equal to zero
21	you are trying to LOAD a no-LOAD file
128	you hit the BREAK key while the machine was doing something
129	the input/output control block already is open
130	you are calling for a nonexistent device
131	you have sent a read command to a write-only device, the printer
132	you can't use that command for that device
133	you forgot to open the file or device
134	that is an illegal device number
135	you are trying to send a write command to a read-only device
136	you have read to the end of the file
137	you are trying to read a record longer than 256 characters
138	the device is turned off, dummy
139	you are getting garbage at a serial port or else you have a bad disk drive
140	input framing error
141	your cursor is out of range for that mode
142	serial bus data frame overrun
143	serial bus data frame checksum error
144	you are trying to write on a write-protected disk

145	something's wrong with what you just wrote
146	that function is not implemented
147	you don't have enough memory available for the graphics mode you selected
160	that's a drive number error
161	you have too many files OPENed
162	the disk is full
163	you've blown the whole bit
164	file numbers don't match, the disk links are messed up
165	that's a file name error
166	there's an error in the POINT data length
167	that file is locked
168	that command is invalid
169	the directory is full
170	that file cannot be located anywhere
171	the POINT is invalid

Appendix C: ASCII Character Numbers

These are the numbers used with the BASIC words ASC and CHR$ to convert to a character or to a number.

For instance, if you write PRINT CHR$(65) the computer will display the upper-case alphabetical letter A. If you were to write PRINT ASC(A) the computer would display the number 65.

Here's the complete list of ASCII character numbers for your ATARI computer:

Decimal Number	Hex Number	Character
0	0	
1	1	

2	2	
3	3	
4	4	
5	5	
6	6	
7	7	
8	8	
9	9	
10	A	
11	B	
12	C	
13	D	
14	E	
15	F	

16	10	
17	11	
18	12	
19	13	
20	14	
21	15	
22	16	
23	17	
24	18	
25	19	
26	1A	
27	1B	
28	1C	
29	1D	

30	1E	←
31	1F	→
32	20	Space
33	21	!
34	22	”
35	23	#
36	24	$
37	25	%
38	26	&
39	27	’
40	28	(
41	29	)
42	2A	*
43	2B	+

44	2C	,
45	2D	-
46	2E	.
47	2F	/
48	30	0
49	31	1
50	32	2
51	33	3
52	34	4
53	35	5
54	36	6
55	37	7
56	38	8
57	39	9

58	3A	:
59	3B	;
60	3C	<
61	3D	=
62	3E	>
63	3F	?
64	40	@
65	41	A
66	42	B
67	43	C
68	44	D
69	45	E
70	46	F
71	47	G

72	48	H
73	49	I
74	4A	J
75	4B	K
76	4C	L
77	4D	M
78	4E	N
79	4F	O
80	50	P
81	51	Q
82	52	R
83	53	S
84	54	T
85	55	U

86	56	V
87	57	W
88	58	X
89	59	Y
90	5A	Z
91	5B	[
92	5C	\
93	5D	]
94	5E	^
95	5F	_
96	60	
97	61	a
98	62	b
99	63	c

100	64	d
101	65	e
102	66	f
103	67	g
104	68	h
105	69	i
106	6A	j
107	6B	k
108	6C	l
109	6D	m
110	6E	n
111	6F	o
112	70	p
113	71	q

114	72	r
115	73	s
116	74	t
117	75	u
118	76	v
119	77	w
120	78	x
121	79	y
122	7A	z
123	7B	
124	7C		
125	7D	
126	7E	
127	7F	
155	9B	(EOL) RETURN
156	9C	
157	9D	
158	9E	
159	9F	

253	FD	 *(Buzzer)*
254	FE	 *(Delete character)*
255	FF	 *(Insert character)*

Books by ARCsoft Publishers

For the TRS-80 PC-1, PC-2, Sharp PC-1211, PC-1500:

99 Tips & Tricks for the New Pocket Computers (PC-2/PC-1500)
128 pages $7.95 ISBN 0-86668-019-5

101 Pocket Computer Programming Tips & Tricks
128 pages $7.95 ISBN 0-86668-004-7

Pocket Computer Programming Made Easy
128 pages $8.95 ISBN 0-86668-009-8

Murder In The Mansion and Other Computer Adventures
96 pages $6.95 ISBN-0-86668-501-4

50 Programs in BASIC for Home, School & Office
96 pages $9.95 ISBN 0-86668-502-2

50 MORE Programs in BASIC for Home, School & Office
96 pages $9.95 ISBN 0-86668-003-9

35 Practical Programs for the Casio Pocket Computer
96 pages $8.95 ISBN 0-86668-014-4

For the TRS-80 Color Computer:

101 Color Computer Programming Tips & Tricks
128 pages $7.95 ISBN 0-86668-007-1

55 Color Computer Programs for Home, School & Office
128 pages $9.95 ISBN 0-86668-005-5

55 MORE Color Computer Programs for Home, School & Office
112 pages $9.95 ISBN 0-86668-008-X

Color Computer Graphics
128 pages $9.95 ISBN 0-86668-012-8

The Color Computer Songbook
96 pages $7.95 ISBN 0-86668-011-X

My Buttons Are Blue and Other Love Poems
96 pages $4.95 ISBN 0-86668-013-6

For the APPLE Computer:

101 APPLE Computer Programming Tips & Tricks
128 pages $8.95 ISBN 0-86668-015-2

33 New APPLE Computer Programs for Home, School & Office
96 pages $8.95 ISBN 0-86668-016-0

For the ATARI 400 and 800 computers:

101 ATARI Computer Programming Tips & Tricks
128 pages $8.95 ISBN 0-86668-022-5

31 New ATARI Computer Programs for Home, School & Office
96 pages $8.95 ISBN 0-86668-018-7

For the Sinclair ZX-81 and TIMEX/Sinclair 1000 computers:

101 TIMEX 1000 and Sinclair ZX-81 Programming Tips & Tricks
128 pages $7.95 ISBN 0-86668-020-9

37 TIMEX 1000 & Sinclair ZX-81 Programs for Home, School & Office
96 pages $8.95 ISBN 0-86668-021-7